CREATE A LIFE YOU LOVE THIS YEAR

CANCELLED

GOODBYE 2020 HELLO 2021

A REFLECTIVE JOURNAL

With special thanks to our wonderful publisher Pavilion – to Laura for designing this beauty and Kom, Cara and Helen for believing in our vision and being an all-round dream to work with. Thank you to our brilliant agent Valeria Huerta and to Fonz, Pav and Sammy for always being on this journey with us.

And a big thank you to our Project Love community for being a constant source of love and inspiration. We love you!

With all our love,

x Selina & Vicki

First published in the United Kingdom in 2020 by
Pavilion
43 Great Ormond Street
London
WC1N 3HZ

Copyright © Pavilion Books Company Ltd 2020
Text copyright © Project Love Ltd 2020

ISBN: 978-1-91166-317-1

A CIP catalogue record for this book is available from the British Library.

10 9 8 7 6 5 4 3 2 1

Reproduction by Rival Colour Ltd, UK
Printed and bound by Toppan Leefung Printing Ltd, China

www.pavilionbooks.com

CREATE A LIFE YOU LOVE THIS YEAR

GOODBYE 2020 HELLO 2021

A REFLECTIVE JOURNAL

Project Love | PAVILION

EVERY NEW BEGINNING COMES FROM SOME OTHER BEGINNING'S END.

Seneca

GOODBYE 2020, HELLO 2021

As one year comes to an end and another begins, it's time for you to take a step back. Pause for a moment in the rush of life and reflect on the year you've just lived – and what a year 2020 has been for all of us around the world.

This year will forever be remembered as the year of Coronavirus. The year when our lives changed dramatically, almost overnight. The year when we collectively went through a challenging and life-changing experience.

In this book we invite you to reflect on what that experience was like for you. It's a chance to recognize and acknowledge all that you've been through and all that you've learnt during this historic year.

And then it's time to close the chapter on 2020 and look to the year that lies ahead. It's time to let yourself dream, to ask yourself what you really want and then, with courage and conviction, commit to making those dreams come true next year.

So let's do that. Let's say goodbye to 2020 and get ready to make 2021 a year to remember!

HOW THIS
JOURNAL WORKS

Goodbye 2020, Hello 2021 guides you through a journey that helps you say a proper farewell to 2020, as it comes to an end, and create a vision and a plan for you to thrive and live a life you love in the year to come.

You'll begin by reflecting on all that has happened in your life in 2020 – your happiest moments, your achievements, the challenges you've overcome and the people you're grateful for. Then, through a series of questions and exercises, you'll be encouraged to think about what you need in life to feel happy, fulfilled and full of love. You'll use those ingredients to choose what you'd most like to focus on in 2021 and which dreams you'd like to bring to life.

By the end of the book, you will have in your hands a vision of the life you want to live in 2021, the dreams you want realized and a simple plan for how you're going to make it all happen.

Goodbye 2020, Hello 2021 will become your motivational journal for designing a life you love in 2021, with quarterly check-ins to help you keep on track throughout the year.

Remember, there is no right or wrong way to answer any of the questions in this book. Relax, have fun with it and just see what answers emerge on the page.

Don't worry if, with some questions, you draw a blank – you can always come back to them later or skip them all together. Not every question will be relevant to you this year.

For every question, you'll find you have a box to fill in with your answer. If you think that you need more space, there are some extra blank pages at the back of the book.

We have loved seeing what *Goodbye, Hello* has done for people over the past nine years and now we can't wait to see what it will do for you!

SHARE WITH US!

There is nothing we love more than seeing photos of you using your *Goodbye, Hello* journals. It is so exciting to see people all over the world dreaming and designing their lives into the pages of this book and sharing their experiences with us.

Share a photo of you doing your *Goodbye, Hello* **journal with us:**

○ @loveprojectlove

#thegoodbyehellojournal

✉ hello@loveprojectlove.com

And look what we've made for you!

A free audio tutorial on '*How to turn your dreams into reality in 2021*'

Come and get it over at
www.thegoodbyehellojournal.com/dreams

x Selina & Vicki

IF A LIFE
WAS A BOOK;
EVERY DAY
WOULD BE
A NEW PAGE,
EVERY MONTH
WOULD BE A
NEW CHAPTER,
AND EVERY
YEAR WOULD
BE A NEW
SERIES.

Elizabeth Duivenvoorde

Goodbye 2020

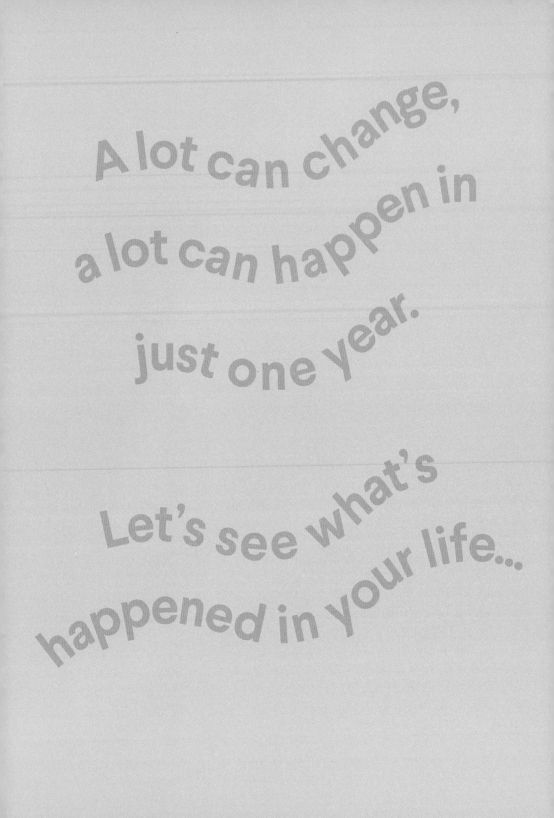

A lot can change,
a lot can happen in
just one year.

Let's see what's
happened in your life...

WHAT HAPPENED IN YOUR LIFE IN 2020?

So, here we are at the end of another year. A life-changing year for everyone on the planet. A year that will go down in global history as a year of change, grief and loss, as well as collective unity, love and hope. And in those 12 months, your life has been a mixture of happy and sad moments, things to celebrate and challenges to overcome. And throughout it all, you have grown and learned in the process.

So now, as we say goodbye to 2020, it's time to take a moment and step back and reflect on how that year has been for you.

If, at first, you find it hard to recall things, then take it slowly. Go month by month, perhaps using your calendar to help remind you of what you got up to over the past year.

We recognize that this is a year when plans were put on hold, dreams had to take a backseat and many of our priorities shifted. This is the time to explore those feelings and frustrations and to turn those emotions into a powerful force for change. Remember that there are no right or wrong answers to any of these questions. You might have just a few lines to write for one question, but with others, you might have so much you want to write that you'll need to use the extra pages at the back of the book.

The key is to relax, spend a little time pondering each question and enjoy this process of reflecting and spending quality time with yourself.

YOUR STORY IS WHAT YOU HAVE, WHAT YOU'WILL ALWAYS HAVE. IT IS SOMETHING TO OWN.

Michelle Obama

What was going on in your life this time last year?

How were you feeling?

As you looked ahead to 2020, what did you want it to be all about for you?

What happened in 2020?

What were the main events and milestones in your life in 2020?

What did you create, achieve and make happen in 2020 (the big and the small)?

WHAT WERE THE MAIN EVENTS AND MILESTONES IN YOUR LIFE IN 2020?

What were your happiest moments?

When did you have the most fun?

When and where did you feel the most at peace?

What has been the most unexpected thing about this year?

What new thing(s) did you discover about yourself?

When did you feel the most love?

What are you particularly proud of?

What have been your hardest moments in 2020?

What have been your biggest challenges?

What are the most important lessons you have learned?

What will 2020 be remembered for in your life?

Gratitude

ACKNOWLEDGING THE GOOD THAT YOU ALREADY HAVE IN YOUR LIFE IS THE FOUNDATION FOR ALL ABUNDANCE.

Eckhart Tolle

THE POWER
OF GRATITUDE

Gratitude is the simple but powerful practice of expressing thanks and giving appreciation for what you have in your life, right now.

Research shows that the practice of gratitude improves your health, increases your happiness and productivity and helps you to foster deep and fulfilling relationships.

At Project Love, we also belive it is a key tool when it comes to designing a life you love, because whatever you focus your attention on, you get more of. Thinking about what you are grateful for, rather than envying what you are lacking, helps to keep you in a positive mindset and the life you dream of feels perfectly possible. Your actions and choices then align with that dream life, help invite it in and make it happen.

Let's create more of what you want in life by taking some time to reflect on all that you're grateful for having in your life right now...

At the moment, what are you grateful for in your life?

Who are you grateful for?

What about yourself are you grateful for this year?

IT IS NOT IN THE STARS TO HOLD OUR DESTINY BUT IN OURSELVES.

William Shakespeare

WHAT DO YOU WANT TO FILL YOUR LIFE WITH?

Now that you've said a proper farewell to 2020, it's time to turn your attention towards 2021. Look at the fresh new canvas ahead of you and choose what you want to fill it with.

In order for you to be able to do that, you first need to be clear on what it is you need in life to feel happy, alive, fulfilled and full of love – this year and beyond. And that is what this next section is all about.

Over the following pages, you're going to build up a juicy list of all the things that make you happy in life: the things you love to do, the people you love to spend your time with and the places you love to spend your time in.

You're going to look back to some of your happiest times in life and the ingredients that helped to make you so happy then and you're going to allow yourself to imagine what you would love your dream life to look like five years from now.

As in the previous section, there are no right or wrong answers to any of these questions. You might have loads to write for one and just a sentence to write on the next. And don't be surprised if you find yourself repeating some answers – this just helps to highlight what is particularly important to you at the moment.

So relax your mind, let your imagination go and see what emerges on the page in front of you as you start to write...

Hello you

GRAB YOUR METAL DETECTOR AND GO DIGGING. UNEARTH NEW PIECES OF TREASURE THAT EXPAND AND NOURISH YOUR SOUL.

@jo_fiddy

What makes you feel happy, alive and fulfilled in life?

WHAT ARE THE THINGS
YOU LOVE TO DO?

What simple pleasures do you enjoy?

What activities make you come alive?

What activities help you to feel calm and relaxed?

What do you love to do on your time off or at weekends?

What do you love to do on holiday?

What are the things that you could spend all day
doing and never get tired of?

What activities do you love to do with the people you love?

What activities do you love to do on your own?

Think back to your happiest moments in life – what were you doing that made you so happy?

WHERE ARE THE PLACES YOU
LOVE TO SPEND TIME IN?

Where do you feel your happiest? (This can be a specific
place, such as at home, or a more general area – by the
sea, for example.)

What places (or kinds of places) do you feel most at
peace and relaxed?

Where are the places that you have the most fun?

What are the kinds of places you like to visit on holiday?

What places in the world would you one day love to visit?

Think back to your happiest moments in life – where were you that made you so happy?

WHO ARE THE PEOPLE YOU
LOVE TO BE WITH?

Who are the people that make you happy in life?

Who are the people you feel most loved by?

Who are the people that inspire you most in life? (You can include people you know, people you follow online or even fictional or historical characters.)

Who are the people you feel you can be most yourself with? And why?

Who are the people that really see your value?

HOW DO YOU LOVE TO FEEL?

When you're at your happiest at home, how do you feel?

When you're at your happiest at work, how do you feel?

When you're at your happiest on your own, how do you feel?

When you're at your happiest among people, how do you feel?

HOW DO YOU LIKE TO
LOOK AFTER YOURSELF?

What helps you to feel good in your body and mind?
E.g. plenty of water, exercise, 8 hours of sleep, yoga,
meditation etc...

What helps to recharge your batteries when you've
tired yourself out?

What life do you dream of?

TAKE YOUR
DREAMS SERIOUSLY

Our ability to dream and then make those dreams happen is the magic we have as human beings.

It is what gives us the power to be able to bring about change in our own lives and in the world around us, and it is therefore a key tool when it comes to designing a life you truly love.

So, over the following few pages, you're going to allow yourself to dream – and dream BIG.

Let yourself imagine that anything is possible and see what dreams emerge when you allow yourself to do that...

DREAMS ARE ILLUSTRATIONS... FROM THE BOOK YOUR SOUL IS WRITING ABOUT YOU.

Marsha Norman

YOUR DREAM LIFE

The key to dreaming and dreaming BIG is to give yourself permission – permission to imagine that anything is possible and to dream from there.

So let's imagine you have a magic wand that you can use to conjure up whatever you want in your own life: your dream home, dream career, dream relationship – whatever it is you want, you can have it.

Now imagine that you're living that life five years from now.

Take yourself there for a moment and describe what that life is like. And don't hold back. Let yourself dream as wildly as your imagination allows...

Where do you live?

What is your home like?

How do you spend your days?

What do you do on your time off?

What kind of holidays do you go on?

Who are the special people in your life?

What have you achieved over the past five years?
(Remember that this is five years into the future.)

Is there anything else you can see in this dream life of yours?

How does it feel to live this life?

What is it that you love the MOST about this life of yours?

THE BIGGEST ADVENTURE YOU CAN EVER TAKE IS TO LIVE THE LIFE OF YOUR DREAMS.

Oprah Winfrey

As you look at your 'dream life', which parts do you want to start introducing the most in 2021?

What practical steps can you take to get started on bringing those dreams to life in 2021?

Hello 2021

THE NEW YEAR STANDS BEFORE US, LIKE A CHAPTER IN A BOOK, WAITING TO BE WRITTEN.

Melody Beattie

HELLO 2021

A fresh new year lies ahead of you. A blank canvas for you to fill with the things you love. A whole new chapter in your life for you to write.

So...what do you want it to be all about? What do you want to fill your life with in 2021? What do you want to make happen? What do you want to experience? How do you want to feel?

It's time to choose.

Creating a life you love is about listening to your dreams, your needs and your desires and then choosing which ones you want to focus on bringing into your life.

As you look back at your answers in this journal so far, it's time to see which dreams are calling to you the most, which ingredients you most want to fill this year with and what you want to choose as your 2021 focus.

Over the following pages, you'll be asked questions designed to help you get clear on what you want to make your 2021 all about.

As with every other section, you will likely find that there are some questions you have clear answers for, while others don't feel so relevant to you this year. Don't worry if you don't have an answer to every question. Just answer the ones that speak to you.

So let's turn the page and start designing your 2021...

WHAT DO YOU WANT TO MAKE YOUR 2021 ALL ABOUT?

Which of your dreams do you want to bring to life this year (or start to bring to life)?

What changes (if any) do you want to make in your life in 2021?

What challenges do you want to take on (if any) in 2021?

How do you want to see yourself grow in 2021?

What else do you want to do or make happen in 2021?

What else do you want your life to be full of
(people, places, activities, holidays, experiences...)?

WHAT DO YOU WANT TO FEEL IN 2021?

Look back at your answers on how you love to feel on page 38 and circle, below, the feelings that call out to you and add any of your own...

Calm, joy, fun, peace, happiness, love,

inspiration, connection, focus,

playfulness, power, contentment, fulfilment,

nourishment, vitality, abundance, freedom,

gratitude, ease, serenity, courage, passion,

stillness, strength, softness, integrity, lightness,

celebration, generosity, balance, kindness,

wonder, commitment, optimism, unity, purpose,

clarity, compassion...

Now circle one to three feelings that you most want to experience in 2021.

In 2021 I want to feel...

What do you want to make your 2021 all about?

THE POWER OF CHOOSING A FOCUS FOR YOUR YEAR

OK, now we are getting to the big moment in your *Goodbye, Hello* journey: it's time for you to choose your focus for the new year.

What do you want to make 2021 all about? What do you want your focus to be?

Having a focus for your year acts like a guiding star, helping to guide your choices and actions in the direction of your dreams.

It is a way for you to commit seriously; to yourself, to your happiness and wellbeing and to creating a life you love.

Over the following pages, you'll find guidance on how to choose your focus, but ultimately it is about choosing a focus that makes you feel good when you imagine a whole year of making that a priority.

So, have a read through of the different ways you can choose your focus, look back over the previous pages in this section and choose a focus that really makes you smile.

WORDS
ARE THE
SPELLS
OF OUR
LIVES

@laurenwallet

HOW TO CHOOSE YOUR FOCUS

The most important thing is that you choose a focus that feels good for you. Never choose a focus for your year because you think you should or because you think it sounds good. Choose a focus for your year that gets you feeling excited and looking forward to the year that lies ahead.

Here are a few different ways you can choose your focus for the year:

Option 1: Choose something that you want more of in your life.

You might be craving more of something in your life like...

Creativity, fun, love, calm, adventure, celebration, nourishment, joy, laughter, peace, clarity, gratitude, self-care, connection, femininity, vitality, self-love, magic.

And so you could make that your focus for 2021 and commit to cultivating more of that into your life in the year to come:

'2021 is my year of fun.'
'2021 is my year of creativity.'
'2021 is my year of self-care.'

Option 2: Choose an intention for the year.

Maybe, as you've been answering the questions in your journal so far, you've felt a desire to set an intention for this year. You might not know how it's going to manifest, but that is part of the magic of it: you set the intention and see how it grows. You just know that this is what you want to make this year all about:

'2021 is my year of stepping into my power.'
'2021 is my year of standing in love.'
'2021 is my year of designing a life I love.'
'2021 is my year of healing.'
'2021 is my year of saying "yes!"'

Option 3: Choose a big change you want to make or a big dream you want to bring to life.

Maybe this is the year when you really feel ready to commit and make that big change happen, or bring that big dream to life. And so that is what you want to choose as your 2021 focus to really fire up your commitment and make it your central focus for the year:

'2021 is my year of starting my own business.'
'2021 is my year of finding an exciting new career path.'
'2021 is my year of buying my first home.'
'2021 is my year of creating my home in a new country.'
'2021 is my year of taking a six-month sabbatical.'

That said, even if you do have a big change you want to make or big dream you want to bring to life in 2021, you don't have to choose that as your focus. You might prefer to focus on how you want to approach making that change. For example, you might want 2021 to be the year that you really get your career change going, but rather than making 2021 your year of 'career change', you might choose to make it your year of 'self-care', to help you focus on looking after your wellbeing while you go through a big life change.

Option 4: Just go with what your gut says.

If you just *know* what you want your focus for 2021 to be, even if it doesn't fit into Options 1 to 3, then go for it. The key with choosing your focus is that it is meaningful and inspiring to *you*.

Now it's time for you to choose a focus for your 2021...

2021
is my year of

....

Why do you want that to be your focus for 2021?

So let's make it happen!

HOW TO DESIGN A LIFE YOU LOVE IN 2021

Designing a life you love doesn't happen by accident. Whatever your dreams, your desires, your visions for this year and the future, it isn't luck that will make them happen. It is you taking action that will ultimately have you creating a life you love.

So now it's time to come up with as many things as you can think of that will help you make 2021 your year of:

....

You can choose big things and small things.

For example, if you chose 2021 to be your year of 'Adventure', then maybe there are a few big adventures you know you want to go on in 2021 or that you already have booked in. Write those down. But don't stop there. What other things could you do to bring adventure into your life this year, even in small ways? Really have some fun with this and, if you struggle to come up with ideas, ask a friend to help brainstorm ideas with you.

On the next page, write down at least 10 things you could do this year to bring your dreams and intentions to life. And do come back to this list and add things to it, as and when you think of them.

All the things I could do, big or small, to make 2021 my year of............................... :

HAPPINESS IS NOT SOMETHING READY MADE. IT COMES FROM YOUR OWN ACTIONS.

Dalai Lama

CHOOSE THREE THINGS TO FOCUS ON FIRST...

Now it's time to choose THREE THINGS that you're going to do between now and April that have you committing to your focus for 2021 and creating a life you love.

Why just three things?

Because we have found over the years that three is the magic number when it comes to setting goals and actually making them happen.

It keeps them memorable and manageable and therefore far more likely to succeed.

Now there is one simple rule to choosing your three commitments; they have to feel good to you. You can stretch yourself with a commitment that kind of scares you (big commitments usually do), but only if the fear is matched with excitement. And no choosing a commitment because you think you should. Designing a life you love will never grow out of doing things just because you think you should.

So choose the three practical steps that appeal to you the most at the moment.

And finally, get specific. If one of your commitments, for example, is to learn Spanish then don't just write down 'I'm going to learn Spanish'. Get specific about how, when and where: 'I'm going to find a Spanish teacher to have a lesson with once a week' or 'I'm going to spend two hours every Wednesday studying Spanish via an online course'.

And then open up your calendar and schedule in the first step you're going to take to get that commitment going (for example, 'research Spanish teachers in my area').

WHAT I WILL DO
JANUARY – MARCH 2021

The three things I commit to doing between now and 31 March:

1.

2.

3.

DECLARE IT

Now that you have your focus for 2021 and your commitments between now and April set, it is time for the final step: to declare your focus and commitments to the world.

Because it is when you start sharing with others what your game plan is for 2021 that the magic really begins. Opportunities start to appear, things seem to align themselves and you'll suddenly begin to notice paths towards your dreams that you might never have thought of before.

So it is time to declare your focus for 2021 to someone in your life. Someone who counts. Someone who loves and supports you and wants to see you live a life you love.

Who will that person be?

....

Let them know what you are committing to doing in 2021 and ask that they hold you to account.

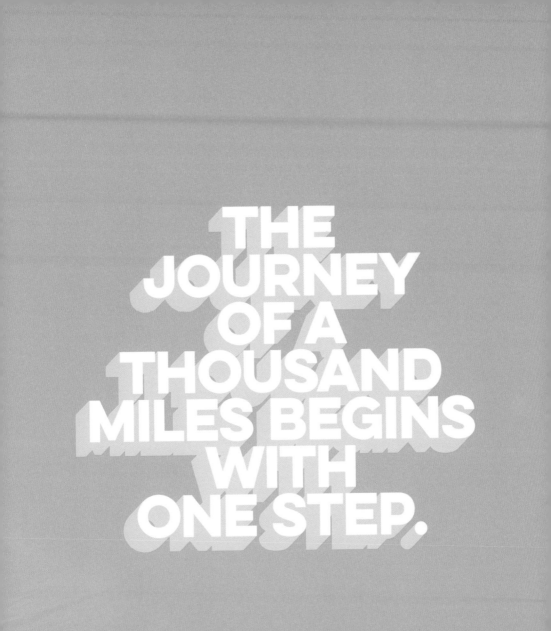

THE JOURNEY OF A THOUSAND MILES BEGINS WITH ONE STEP.

Lao Tzu

A MESSAGE FROM YOU TO YOU

Learning to give yourself the words of encouragement and support you need to help you go forwards into the world and create a life you love is every bit as important as creating a plan and action steps that will bring those dreams to life.

However, most of us tend to be our own harshest critics and we are more tuned into the negative, critical side of ourselves that is ready to point out where we're failing and cast doubt over whether we really have what it takes to make our dreams happen. We often only use our loving supportive side on our loved ones. Now it's time to turn that loving attention towards yourself.

Let that side of you write a message of encouragement to you as you step into 2021, ready to make you and your happiness a top priority and ready to create a life you love...

My message from me to me...

And so the
journey begins...

STOP WATCHING FROM THE SIDELINES. START NOW AND GO AFTER YOUR DREAMS.

@drtilean

Designing a life you love in 2021

DESIGNING A LIFE YOU LOVE IN 2021

One of the main problems with our traditional New Year's resolutions is that we create a list of the things we'd like to achieve over the course of the year, get excited about it and then, by the time we've hit February, we're so caught up in the rush of life that our sparkly list of New Year's resolutions has been pretty much forgotten.

According to research, only 8% of New Year's resolutions ever happen and 50% fail within the first month.

So, with *Goodbye, Hello* we do things differently.

We get you to hold onto just one main focus for the year and then commit to doing just three things every three months that will help you to stick to your focus for 2021 and design a life you love.

At the start of every quarter (that is, the start of April, July and October) we bring you back to your *Goodbye, Hello* journal so that you can check in with yourself, reflect on the previous three months and revisit your three commitments to see how you got on.

You then set three fresh new commitments for the following three months; commitments that support you in creating a life that you love.

Come and follow us over on Instagram and we'll remind you at the start of each quarter when it's time for your quarterly check-in.

⊙ @loveprojectlove

Living a life you love doesn't happen by accident.

It isn't down to luck.

It's down to you.

Remind yourself of your dreams on a regular basis and keep taking practical steps until you've made those dreams come true.

Quarterly check-ins

STRIPPED
BACK IS
WHERE WE
MEET
OURSELVES.

@jessica_huie_

April

It's time to take a step back and review how things have been going over the past three months. What have you been up to? Have you been making time in your life for the things that are most important to you? Have you been doing things to bring to life your focus for 2021? How did you get on with your three commitments? Let's take a look... and if you want to do your review together with us then tune into the Project Love podcast.

How are you feeling at the moment?

What has happened in your life since January?

What have you done that you're proud of?

What have been your happiest moments?

What have been your most challenging moments?

What and who are you grateful for at this moment in your life?

APRIL CHECK-IN

Go and take a look at your focus for 2021 and the three things you committed to doing. It's time to review how things have been going:

What have you done from that list of commitments?

What haven't you done from that list of commitments?

If there is anything you didn't do from that list of commitments then what do you think has got in the way of you doing it?

Do you want to carry this commitment through to the next quarter? If you do, then what can you do to make sure you prioritize it between now and 30 June?

Take a moment to remind yourself of your focus for 2021 and return to the list you made on p.66. What on that list appeals to you the most right now? Is there anything you want to add to it?

Now choose the THREE THINGS you most want to commit to doing over the next three months and write them down on the next page.

WHAT I WILL DO
APRIL – JUNE 2021

The three things I commit to doing between now and 30 June:

1.

2.

3.

LIKE LEOPARD PRINT, JOY IS A NEUTRAL, IT GOES WITH EVERYTHING.

@livethreesixty

July

JULY REFLECTIONS

It's time to take a step back and review how things have been going over the past three months. What have you been up to? Have you been making time in your life for the things that are most important to you? Have you been doing things to bring to life your focus for 2021? How did you get on with your three commitments? Let's take a look... and if you want to do your review together with us then tune into the Project Love podcast.

How are you feeling at the moment?

What has happened in your life since April?

What have you done that you're proud of?

What have been your happiest moments?

What have been your most challenging moments?

What and who are you grateful for at this moment in your life?

JULY CHECK-IN

Go and take a look at your focus for 2021 and the three practical steps you committed to taking between April and now. It's time to review how things have been going:

What have you done from that list of commitments?

What haven't you done from that list of commitments?

If there is anything you didn't do from that list of commitments, then what do you think has got in the way of you doing it?

Do you want to carry this commitment through to the next quarter? If you do, then what can you do to make sure you prioritize it between now and 30 September?

Take a moment to remind yourself of your focus for 2021 and return to the list you made on p.66. What on that list appeals to you the most right now? Is there anything you want to add to it?

Now choose the THREE THINGS you most want to commit to doing over the next three months and write them down on the next page.

WHAT I WILL DO
JULY – SEPTEMBER 2021

The three things I commit to doing between now and 30 September.

1.

2.

3.

YOU ARE BRAVER THAN YOU BELIEVE, STRONGER THAN YOU SEEM, AND SMARTER THAN YOU THINK.

Winnie the Pooh

October

OCTOBER REFLECTIONS

It's time to take a step back and review how things have been going over the past three months. What have you been up to? Have you been making time in your life for the things that are most important to you? Have you been doing things to bring to life your focus for 2021? How did you get on with your three commitments? Let's take a look... and if you want to do your review together with us then tune into the Project Love podcast.

How are you feeling at the moment?

What has happened in your life since July?

What have you done that you're proud of?

What have been your happiest moments?

What have been your most challenging moments?

What and who are you grateful for at this moment in your life?

Go and take a look at your focus for 2021 and the three practical steps you committed to taking between 1 July and now. It's time to review how things have been going:

What have you done from that list of commitments?

What haven't you done from that list of commitments?

If there is anything you didn't do from that list of commitments, then what do you think has got in the way of you doing it?

Do you want to carry this commitment through to the next quarter? If you do, then what can you do to make sure you prioritize it between now and 31 December?

Take a moment to remind yourself of your focus for 2021 and return to the list you made on p.66. What on that list appeals to you the most right now? Is there anything you want to add to it?

Now choose the THREE THINGS you most want to commit to doing over the next three months and write them down on the next page.

WHAT I WILL DO
OCTOBER – DECEMBER 2021

The three things I commit to doing between now and 31 December:

1.

2.

3.

TO BE YOURSELF IN A WORLD THAT IS CONSTANTLY TRYING TO MAKE YOU SOMETHING ELSE IS THE GREATEST ACCOMPLISHMENT.

Ralph Waldo Emerson

Time to reflect on 2021

A FINAL REFLECTION

And so we've come to the end of another year. It is time to take a step back and reflect on all that has happened in 2021 and, in particular, on which of the intentions and dreams written into the pages of this journal have become a reality in your life this past year.

Now, not all of those inentions and dreams will have materialised and that's OK. Some dream seeds grow and flourish and others don't.

For now, we want you to reflect on the dreams written into this journal that *did* come true in 2021 and how having a focus for your year helped you to flourish.

So let's start by taking a look at your focus for 2021.

2021 was my year of ....

What has it been like to have this as your focus for
a year?

How did you help to make your 2021 about that?

Read through page 48 and pages 52-54 and take a look at the dreams you wanted to bring to life, the changes you wanted to make, how you wanted to grow and what you wanted to make happen in 2021.

Which of the things you wrote down *did* happen this year?

Is there anything you wrote down that didn't happen this year and you wish it had?

What can you do to help make that happen in 2022?

As you look back on 2021 and the dreams *you* brought to life and the intentions that shaped your year, take a moment to celebrate yourself. Celebrate your power to create your own reality and your ability to bring your dreams to life and to materialise the changes you wanted to see in your own life and the world around you.

How does it feel to know that you can be the artist of your own life and are taking steps, big and small, to create the life you want to be living?

GOODBYE FOR NOW

And so with that, your *Goodbye 2020, Hello 2021* journey is complete!

Forgive yourself if there were any dreams, intentions or commitments that you didn't bring to life this year. It's not about getting a perfect score (not at all!). Instead, focus on what you did create and make happen in your life. And celebrate!

Life design, at its core, is about recognising that you have the power to be the artist of your own life. You possess the magic that all human beings have, of being able to make your dreams a reality.

All it takes is the willingness to allow yourself to dream, take those dreams seriously and turn them into projects and actions that, step by step, will bring those dreams to life.

So grab a hold of that magic that you possess and we'll see you over in the *Goodbye 2021, Hello 2022 journal* for another year of creating a life you love!

With all our love,

x Selina & Vicki

KEEP AN EYE ON **THEGOODBYEHELLOJOURNAL.COM**
TO LOOK FOR UPDATES ON THE NEXT GOODBYE, HELLO JOURNAL